C000171686

20th Century Passenger Flying Boats

20th Century Passenger Flying Boats

Leslie Dawson

Pen & Sword
AVIATION

AN IMPRINT OF PEN & SWORD BOOKS LTD
YORKSHIRE – PHILADELPHIA

First published in Great Britain in 2021 by
PEN & SWORD AVIATION
An imprint of
Pen & Sword Books Ltd
Yorkshire – Philadelphia

Copyright © Leslie Dawson, 2021

ISBN 978 1 52674 420 3

The right of Leslie Dawson to be identified
as Author of this work has been asserted by him in accordance
with the Copyright, Designs and Patents Act 1988.

A CIP catalogue entry for this book is available from the British Library.
All rights reserved. No part of this book may be reproduced
or transmitted in any form or by any means, electronic
or mechanical including photocopying, recording or by any information
storage and retrieval system, without permission from the Publisher in writing.

Printed and bound by CPI Group (UK) Ltd, Croydon, CR0 4YY
Typeset in Ehrhardt MT Std 11.5/14 by
SJmagic DESIGN SERVICES, India.

Pen & Sword Books Ltd includes the Imprints of
Atlas, Archaeology, Aviation, Discovery, Family History, Fiction, History, Maritime,
Military, Military Classics, Politics, Select, Airworld, Frontline Publishing, Leo Cooper,
Remember When, Seaforth Publishing, The Praetorian Press, Wharncliffe Local History,
Wharncliffe Transport, Wharncliffe True Crime and White Owl.

For a complete list of Pen & Sword titles please contact
PEN & SWORD BOOKS LIMITED
47 Church Street, Barnsley, South Yorkshire, S70 2AS, England
E-Mail: enquiries@pen-and-sword.co.uk * Website: www.pen-and-sword.co.uk

Or

PEN AND SWORD BOOKS
1950 Lawrence Rd, Havertown, PA 19083, USA
E-mail: Uspen-and-sword@casematepublishers.com
Website: www.penandswordbooks.com

Contents

A huge debt of thanks is owed to the many private and public photo collections who kindly contributed to this tribute to a memorable form of air travel.

Leslie Dawson
Bournemouth
England

The First

Having previously failed, despite coupling three engines to a propeller, Henri Fabre fitted aerodynamic floats to a new design, *Le Canard*, which, on 28 March 1910, became the first to leave water (the Étang de Berre near Marseille) under its own power.

In May 2010 a full-size replica, built by Guillaume Bulin and Marc Anscieau, was displayed at Lake Biscarosse, home of the Musée de l'Hydraviation, to mark the centenary.

Glenn Curtiss was the first American to use ailerons rather than wing warping and was honoured for developing the 'hydro-aeroplane'. His 1912 model E featured a hull instead of mounting a landplane on floats, with a 'step' to reduce the area in contact with the surface. The F had a V-shaped hull. He is acknowledged as creating the first practical flying boat.

Glenn Curtiss. (© Marc Fabre)

The world's first scheduled passenger flight was made on 1 January 1914 by the Benoist XIV 'airboat' *Lark of Duluth* for the St Petersburg-Tampa Air Boat Line. By the end of March, *Lark of Duluth* and *Florida* had carried over 1,200 passengers at $5 a time – the birth of commercial aviation.

Le Canard replica, Biscarosse, 2010. (© David Barrie)

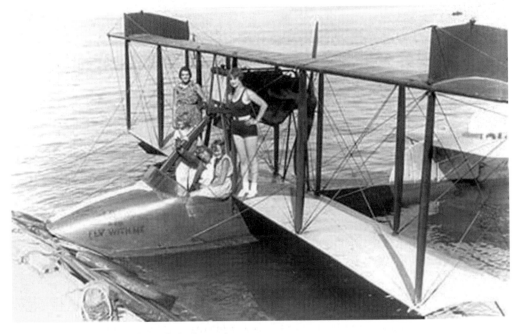

Curtiss MF (modified F) Seagull. (unknown)

Tony Jannus landing at Duluth in 1914. (© Alan Radecki, The Mojave West Vintage Photo Archive)

A replica of *Lark of Duluth* at St Petersburg–Clearwater International Airport, Florida. (© Joe May/ Travel for Aircraft)

Great Britain

John Porte worked with Curtiss on a contender for a non-stop Atlantic flight and recommended Curtiss flying boats for the Royal Naval Air Service. Given command of the Seaplane Experimental Establishment at Felixstowe, his modifications improved the water handling of the American flying boats. His Felixstowe design served the RNAS and the RAF, and was modified by Curtiss for the US Navy. He is considered Britain's greatest flying-boat pioneer.

Supermarine (former Admiralty Department) Channel flying boats delivered newspapers and gave pleasure flights from Southampton, Bournemouth and the Isle of Wight. A summer 1919 trip round Bournemouth Bay cost three guineas but, with her father employed in ferrying passengers from the pier to the mooring, Agnes Allen and her fiancé William Fyson were given a free flight.

The first scheduled passenger service by a British flying boat was made on 25 September 1923 during the inaugural Southampton-Guernsey service of the

Wealthy Australian Lebbeus Hordern bought a pair of Curtiss Seagulls and this Short-built Felixstowe 'Air Yacht'. (© Shorts [Bombardier] Publicity Department, Belfast)

(© William and
Agnes Fyson)

(Courtesy of the Roy Tassell Collection)

British Marine Air Navigation Company. Created by Reginald J. Mitchell, remembered more for his Schneider Trophy winners and legendary Spitfire, the Supermarine Sea Eagle had two large wheels to roll ashore. On 1 April 1924, the company was absorbed within Imperial Airways.

Long-Distance Pioneer

Former wartime pilot Alan Cobham met his wife, actress Gladys Lloyd, while flying 'joy rides' in Yorkshire before joining the de Havilland Aircraft Company.

South Africa was a particular goal of the airlines. In 1926 he made the first return flight to Capetown, and Australia. He was subsequently knighted.

(© Flight Refuelling Ltd)

Australia. (From the album of Jack Nolan RAF, courtesy of Martin Wilkinson)

A clockwise survey of Africa aboard a Short Singapore flying boat ended in June 1928. But in December the government bought out Cobham-Blackburn Airlines, formed to operate flying-boat services between Alexandria and Capetown, in favour of Imperial Airways.

The first to make aviation available to the general public, Sir Alan Cobham's Air Display gave many their very first flight.

Right: Short Singapore.

Below: Air Display en route to another venue. (© Flight Refuelling Ltd)

Kent Class

From 1931, Imperial Airways Kent-class flying boats crossed the Mediterranean between Mirabella in Crete and Alexandria, the luxurious accommodation soon becoming associated with all flying-boat services.

Satyrus, Lake Tiberius, circa 1935.

15-seat cabin. (© Eric and Edith Matson photographs, Library of Congress)

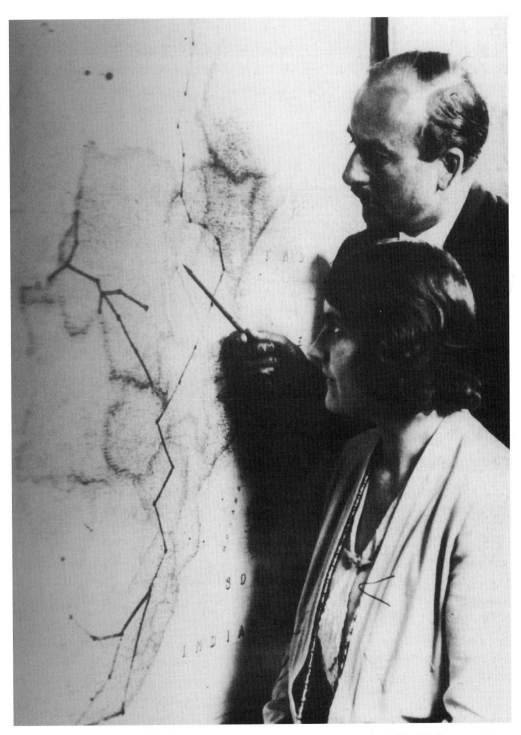

Sir Alan and Lady Cobham peruse a map of African air routes. (© Flight Refuelling Ltd)

Empire flying boats

Britain's famous flying-boat era was a direct result of the Empire Air Mail Postal Scheme, created to send a half-ounce (14-gram) letter to anywhere in the British Empire for the same penny-halfpenny (0.5p) stamp required for everyday letters.

Short Brothers received a £1.25 million order for twenty-eight flying boats. *Canopus*, the first of the Empire- or C-class fleet, flew from the Medway in July 1936. The service opened formally to the Sudan, East and South Africa in June 1937. Over forty aircraft were built subsequently.

(© Short Brothers)

(Courtesy of Adrian Meredith photography)

C-class to Africa

The Africa service was a success from the start. Having paid £125 for your flight to Durban you receive a gold-edged card confirming the booking. Arriving at the Empire Terminal Building in Buckingham Palace Road, and having had your weight taken and that of your luggage, you are passed through to the adjoining railway platform reserved for Imperial Airways. A noticeboard proclaims the Empire Air Service and the name of the Royal Mail aircraft while the hands of a small clock face show the departure time with the platform number chalked beneath. Two Pullman carriages at the rear of the train repeat the name of the flying boat and the sound of whistles heralds the start of your adventure.

A comfortable journey ends at the Southampton Flying Boat Terminal where an airline traffic officer conducts you aboard a coach to take you to the South Western Hotel. On entering you receive a little card which, among other things, says you will be called at 4 o'clock in the morning! Only half-awake at that hour, armed with your inoculation certificate, airline ticket and stiff-backed British passport, the coach takes you to the dockside terminal. After completing the paperwork, you wait in the lounge until the flying boat is ready to receive passengers, when you are conducted onto a gangway leading to the pontoon.

The bow of the flying boat is secured to a buoy in the Solent, with mooring lines run from bollards to recessed cleats on both sides of the opened entry doors. With navigation and interior lights all switched on, the aircraft brightens an otherwise drab British dockside. Aware of the cables to the tail hook, and passing the unblinking tail light, you find the words 'Royal Air Mail' printed in a semi-circle on the fuselage. The nearest door leads into the promenade cabin, but you are allowed entry from the nose hatch to have a good look at the interior. Glancing above, you see the Civil Air Ensign and triangular pennant of the Royal Mail on the flag staff behind the aerial mast.

Stepping down from the gently swaying pontoon, you enter the metal 'lobby' with a drawn-aside curtain and vertical flight-deck ladder. On the left, the open door of the smokers' cabin (cigarettes only) reveals a curving roof and light-green walls, viewing ports with roller blinds, Pullman-style seats and fold-back tables. The wall lights have an extra button to summon the steward. Both sides have cord-strung, Pullman-style hat-racks while recessed metal compartments stow overnight bags. Handles mark the door to the mooring compartment.

Moving past the toilets and pantry, you enter the smaller centre cabin. Both sides have three viewing ports with two of the three seats on the right. A step then takes you

BOAC Solent with air mail. Southampton, 1950.
(© Royal Mail Group 2019, courtesy of The Postal Museum p118/2016)

Southampton,
circa 1938.
(© *The Aeroplane*)

up into the much publicised promenade cabin, though not without noticing the little sign placed above every door to remind passengers that there was to be no smoking. Aside from three pairs of seats and tables on the left, the aisle features four large viewing ports with taut sliding curtains and a long slender handrail.

The far (main) entrance door has a viewing port to avoid a watery exit. Two steps take you up into the aft cabin, fitted with a pair of facing seats to the left, two facing pairs on the right, fold-back tables, and three viewing ports on each side. Flights ended in daylight or late evening, which was fortunate, for the movement made entering the converted bunk beds difficult, particularly when mounting the short ladder. At the final bulkhead, handles mark the door to the freight and baggage compartment, loaded externally from the starboard side. On your way, you had appreciated the regular positioning of Pyrene fire extinguishers, the steadying hand rail at each cabin door, and the fitted carpet beneath your feet.

With your name checked off his list by the flight clerk, who has relieved you of your passport and paperwork, you are shown to your seat by the steward, who deftly shows how five simultaneous movements of the arm levers takes you to the reclining position (not during take off or landing) and how to secure the straps. After asking whether you would like a rug or a foot muff he moves on, leaving you to settle into the comfortable green upholstery, your body beginning to attune, like a sailor, to the restless pitching of the hull.

The closing of the doors against the rubber sealing gaskets is followed by whistles ordering the release of the ropes. The tail hook is freed and the captain and first officer begin the starting of engines. Though forewarned by the steward, the sudden sound and vibration, accompanied by brief bursts of flame, momentarily ends conversation as each metal propeller is forced into action. With all four engines running smoothly, the big aircraft begins to move: the water slapping against the hull beneath your feet just another sensation to get used to.

There is no running up of engines on the brakes as with a landplane, however. There are no brakes, just an advance of throttles in pairs while moving towards Calshot and a large area reserved off the Netley shore to avoid conflict with the ocean liners. The turning into wind is followed by a high-pitched whine and rumble as a motor extends the under-wing flaps and, at exactly 5.30 am, the first officer triggers the Aldis lamp to request take off from the control launch. The steady white light in reply brings a booming roar as the propellers disappear and spray covers the windows.

A flat calm requires a much longer distance to rise on to the 'step', whereas today's light chop has helped break the surface tension. The crew are absorbed by the sound of the engines, while those below can only listen to the rapid increase in frequency of the staccato slaps as the hull is thrown against the water. A similar situation exists on landing, when a crew's 'smooth', perhaps 'classic', view of their pilot's return to the water is felt by those seated on the lower deck as a definite 'thud' as the hull takes the initial shock.

The engine note deepens as the hull breaks free of the foaming water and is held level to establish precious knots before climbing away. Time for the radio operator to trail his aerial to inform the next ground station of the time of take off, destination and estimated time of arrival – in code. A reduction in power coincides with reaching the cruising altitude, when the whining motor returns the grumbling metal under the wings.

Based on the previous day's information, which includes the tide and water states, the captain has chosen one of four main routes. The northernmost pair turn over the Nab Tower Lighthouse, off the east coast of the Isle of Wight, before heading for Fécamp or le Havre. The southerly pair turn over Calshot to head for the Needles, off the western extremity of the island, making landfall either to the right of the lighthouse at Pointe de Barfleur or at Dinard, having overflown the Channel Islands.

The drone of the engines holds your thoughts until you are offered an English breakfast and coffee served by the attendant steward. Most of the flight is below 10,000 feet and in sight of land or water, the wide river valleys, large forests and coastal estuaries confirming the aircraft's position to the crew. Deciding to stretch your legs, you move to the promenade cabin and lean on the rail to watch the changing landscape as the wide Garonne is succeeded by the winding Tarn. In the distance the Alps retain their customary wisps of cloud.

Descending towards the clear waters of Lake Marignane, the landing ends with a turn toward the jetty and you can either relax in the warmth, watching landplanes circuiting the nearby aerodrome, or take a seat in the lounge shared with Ala Littoria. The refuelling and exchange of mail completed, the French Riviera steadily recedes as you pass deeper into the Mediterranean, making landfall above the island of Corsica and crossing the Tyrrhenian Sea to the Italian mainland and Lake Bracciano. The terminal building, Idroscalo Civile, is backed by wooded olive groves rising to the medieval hilltop fortress of Bracciano castle and the comfortable lounge is again shared with the Italian airline.

On your return you notice that the Italian flag has been added to the mast, the now familiar spray of foam accompanying the take-off before climbing to head for Brindisi, to the east of the Gulf of Taranto. The captain flies across Italy via Benevento rather than waste fuel by climbing to the 10,000 feet required to directly approach the Italian naval base. At midday, the white-coated steward transforms the baize-covered tables for lunch, the white linen and silver-service cutlery topped off by a small posy of fresh flowers. As with ocean liners, the tables have a raised metal rim to avoid accidents.

The crew are served by tray at their stations. Should either pilot decide on a full meal, the steward sets the centre cabin (fitted with a clock and altimeter) where a celebrity might be invited to join the 'Captain's table'. The steward is constantly on the move, for each press of a button lights a coloured bulb on a wall panel in his pantry.

Losing height over the low-lying plain bordering the Adriatic, dotted with olive groves and citrus trees, you near the breakwater of Brindisi Harbour. Cameras have been collected by the clerk and placed in a sealed bag until customs are cleared. An Ala Littoria launch arrives alongside and you again use the lounge of the airline. Back aboard, you cross the Straits of Otranto in the late afternoon and make landfall above the island of Corfu before crossing the mountainous Greek mainland to the Gulf of Corinth.

The landing at Phaleron Bay is made almost at dusk and the night is spent at the Hotel Grande Bretagne, where the 4.15 Saturday morning call seems easier to contemplate than in Britain. Luggage will be collected from outside the door half an hour later and cars will arrive at 5.15 to take you to the refuelled and mailed-up aircraft for a 6.00 am departure. Breakfast and lunch will be served in the air.

The early morning sun warms the senses as the aircraft climbs over an island-studded sea before crossing the Mediterranean to North Africa and Alexandria Harbour, the end of the line for the Calcutta- and Kent-class. The day now ends at Rod-el-Farag on the Nile, with an overnight stay in the Egyptian capital of Cairo (al-Qāhirah). A coach takes you to Shepheard's Hotel, a favourite haunt of the rich and famous, though the driver might equally have drawn up at the Continental Savoy. Refreshed and airborne again, with perhaps half the passengers transferred to the Australian service, you watch the changing landscape of East Africa as you follow the Blue Nile to Luxor for another overnight stay.

The following day you reach Wadi Halfa, on the Egyptian border, emerging into a wall of heat which continues unabated to Khartoum in Sudan, where you alight to a moored houseboat before spending the night at the Grand Hotel. Driven to the quayside by an Imperial Airways bus after an early breakfast, the next landing is made on a straight stretch of the Nile at Malakal, where dug-out canoes approach the aircraft, paddled from their riverside village by surprisingly tall members of the Shilluk tribe.

By now you have come to feel an association and affection for this flying boat which, amid an unforgettable mixture of hot metal and aviation spirits, has provided a host of memories. At every refuelling and oiling stop, your smartly-attired companions have been offered coffee or iced tea and cakes as the mail is unloaded and fresh mail taken aboard. Passenger launches approached with care, as did the long refuelling barges overseen by pith-helmeted engineers.

Though fascinating to contrast the lush green surrounding the irrigation ditches bordering the Nile with the desert stretching into the distance, flying at such low levels could bring unexpected detours to avoid dust-storms and swarms of locusts. The waters of the Nile are well up, however, enabling a refuelling stop at Juba, Southern Sudan, rather than the more southerly Rijaf. Landings are made at Laropi and Port Bell on the vast expanse of Lake Victoria where a coach takes you to a hotel at Kampala.

In the morning a large brass bell is struck to announce the departure for Kisumu, Kenya, the desert sands replaced by swampland, small tributaries and glistening lakes before descending for a night's rest at the Kisumu Hotel. Each flying boat has its own

Above left: Promenade cabin, *Caledonia*. (© British Airways)

Above right: Rod el Farag on the Nile. (© Jack Harris collection)

S–33 *Cleopatra*, last of the Empires, refuelling at Malindi. (© Flight Refuelling)

Houseboat *Richard King*. (© Rose collection)

stationery and the captain signs certificates after crossing the Equator. Folders have potted histories of the regions below and captains often circle over places of interest such as the Indian palaces, the pyramids of Egypt, the cascading Nile at Murchison Falls – even large herds of game animals.

Leaving Kisumu behind, you fly across Kenya towards the east coast and Mombasa, landing at Dar es Salaam and Lindi, before passing the sedimental delta of the Rovuma river (Cape Delgardo) on the edge of the Indian Ocean. The day ends at Mozambique Island with an overnight stop at Lumbo. The crew lodge in the houseboat *Richard King*. Then on to Beira and Lourenço Marques in the morning, before descending to follow the coast line where large shoals of fish, even sharks, are visible in the clear waters about the reefs and islands.

The arrival of the steward to ensure everyone is strapped in their seats heralds the approach to Durban, named after a governor of the Cape Colony. Launches ferry everyone ashore and, after saying your goodbyes on the quayside, you take a rather wistful look back at the flying boat, where the national flag is displayed and each propeller has been turned over to leave one blade vertical – as you had found at Southampton, five days and over 7,000 miles away.

The Atlantic

Unable to attract support from the government of Brazil, on 28 April 1927, Jahú-born, 23-year-old João Ribierro de Barros and his crew made a heroic rain-lashed private non-stop crossing of the Atlantic between Cape Verde and the island of Fernando de Noronha, aboard a second-hand Savoia-Marchetti S.55 flying boat. A tour of honour to São Paulo, via Natal, Recife, Salvador and Rio de Janeiro, ended on the Santo Amaro Dam in August. João is remembered by a fine statue, mausoleum and a major highway, his numerous awards held by the Aeronautics Museum, São Paulo. 'Jahú' has been preserved for posterity.

Above: Engines ready for inspection, Santo Amaro dam.

Left: Talking to admirers, São Paulo.

Campos Square Siqueira. (© Alex Rodrigues)

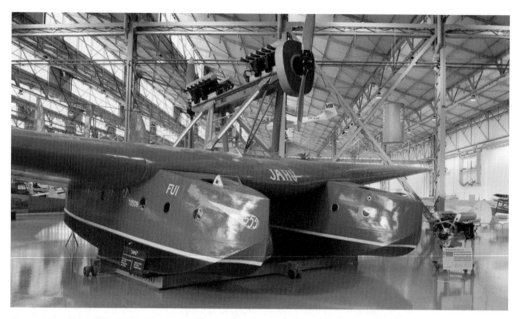

Aeronautics Museum. (© Marcelo Bordim)

Looped hose

Sir Alan Cobham experimented with in-flight refuelling from his former Flying Circus base at Ford Aerodrome, near Littlehampton, where a weighted line trailed from a Handley Page tanker was caught by a shepherd's crook from an Airspeed Courier.

Sir Alan Cobham memorial, Scott USAF base, Illinois. (Courtesy of Airlift/ Tanker Association)

Harrow refuelling *Cabot*. (Photo © Flight Refuelling Ltd)

His Flight Refuelling Company subsequently fired a cable from a Harrow tanker across a cable trailed by an Empire flying boat. Cable and fuel hose were then retrieved by the flying boat to begin the transfer of 800 gallons of petrol, preceded by a supply of nitrogen to avoid an electrical discharge. Flight-refuelled Southampton–New York airmail flights were made during August and September 1939.

Maia and *Mercury*

With Imperial Airways about to undertake trial crossings of the North Atlantic, technical manager Major Robert Mayo combined with Short Brothers in producing the Short Mayo Composite. In July 1938 Donald Bennett flew *Mercury* from Foynes to Boucherville, Montreal, in twenty hours and twenty minutes.

The increase in scale for a passenger version proved impracticable, but the idea was revived in the 1970s when Boeing 747s carried the NASA space shuttle between launch and landing areas. By then, the 'looped hose' system had been adapted for military refuelling and, in 1982, took Vulcan XM607 to the Falklands during the longest bombing raid in history.

Assembling *Mercury* (on top) and *Maia* for flight, Foynes.
(© Foynes Flying Boat Museum)

G-class

Pictured on Shorts' slipway, *Golden Hind* was the first of three S-26 flying boats designed to cross the North Atlantic non-stop in association with the Pan Am Clippers.

(© Public Record Office of Northern Ireland)

Golden Fleece during refitting for military service. (© Short Bros and Harland)

The war ended the Atlantic hopes of Imperial Airways and Air France. Pan Am services ended at Foynes, in neutral Ireland. *Golden Hind, Golden Fleece* and *Golden Horn* entered the RAF as the G–class.

America

Model 75 Aeromarine factory, Keyport, New Jersey c. 1923. (© timetableimages)

The first daily scheduled international passenger/airmail service in America was flown between Key West and Havana, Cuba, by Aeromarine West Indies Airways from November 1920; the two former military Curtiss flying boats modified by the Aeromarine Plane and Motor Company as the Model 75. Aeromarine Airways services increased, using eleven-seat 75s and six-seat Model 85s, until 1924, by which time over 17,000 passengers had enjoyed the experience, particularly those escaping prohibition.

Sikorsky

Pan American Airways operated Sikorsky S-38 flying boats between Miami and Central America. Private customers included the wildlife photographers and pilots Martin and Osa Johnson, their S-38 *Osa's Ark* and single-engined S-39 *Spirit of Africa* respectively given zebra stripes and giraffe spots. Their fifth 1933/34 safari featured aerial pictures of game herds and they were the first to film Mount Kilimanjaro and Mount Kenya from the air.

Martin and Osa with *Osa's Ark*.

Jungle airstrip with Osa in foreground. (© The Martin and Osa Johnson Safari Museum, Chanute, Kansas)

Probably taken at Dinner
Key, Miami. (© Smithsonian
National Air and Space Museum
(NASM 2000-6129))

First 'Flying Clipper'

Introduced in November 1931, Pan Am's trio of Sikorsky S-40s were the first to be
named 'Clipper' after the China-tea sailing ships of the 1860s. They featured a buffet
and smokers' cabin.

Martin Ocean Transports

Designed for the Pacific, Pan Am's three Martin M-130 flying boats began a five-day
service from San Francisco to Manila from October 1936, the year the film *China
Clipper* portrayed the driving force of Juan Trippe, starring a young Humphrey Bogart.

Hawaii Clipper. (© courtesy of the Hawaii State Archives)

Douglas Dolphin

Developed from an 'air yacht' design, bought by Bill Boeing among others, from 1934 a pair of six-seat Douglas Dolphin amphibians was operated by the Chinese National Aviation Company (part owned by Pan Am) between Hong Kong and the Chinese mainland. Others served the US Army, Navy and Coast Guard.

(© Michael Smith, grandson of Captain Edward Smith)

Samoan Clipper and
Imperial Airways
Centaurus, Mechanics
Bay, Auckland, 1937.
(© Alexander Turnbull
Library 1/4-048844-G)

Sikorsky S-42

Built specifically for Pan Am as an improvement on the S-40, S-42s were flown
primarily between Miami and Rio de Janeiro. In March 1937 New Zealand welcomed
Samoan Clipper to Auckland at the end of a proving flight from San Francisco.

Boeing 314

The largest civil aircraft of its time, so clean was its design that the rudder had
insufficient air to function and was replaced by triple fins and two rudders. In June 1939

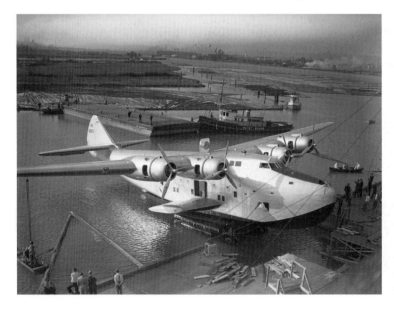

Prototype *Honolulu
Clipper* with single fin.
(© Boeing)

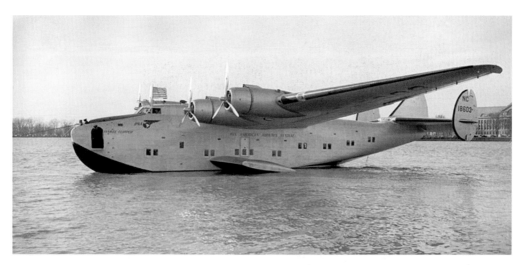

Yankee Clipper, circa 1939. (© Harris and Ewing Collection, Library of Congress)

Dixie Clipper inaugurated the passenger service to Marseilles, via the Azores and Lisbon, and in July *Yankee Clipper* flew the first direct New York-Foynes service.

Sikorsky VS-44A

In 1940 the American Export Airline was awarded a seven-year contract to fly to Lisbon with the Sikorsky VS-44A, designed specifically to compete with the Boeing Clippers. In January 1942 AEA began flying between La Guardia, New York, and Foynes for the US Navy Air Transport Service, the politicians, entertainers and diplomats being flown at night to avoid the Luftwaffe.

Excambian. (© New England Air Museum)

France

The 1938 French Air Ministry specification required an aircraft capable of flying forty passengers and mail for over 3,700 miles. The Latécoère 631 flew in 1942 but was taken over by the Luftwaffe. A second was completed in 1943 but was dismantled before the Resistance blew up the factory. *Lionel de Marmier* finally flew in 1945, hailed as the world's largest commercial flying boat.

Lionel de Marmier. Cockpit painting by Georges Hamel. (Courtesy of Jean Paul HUG)

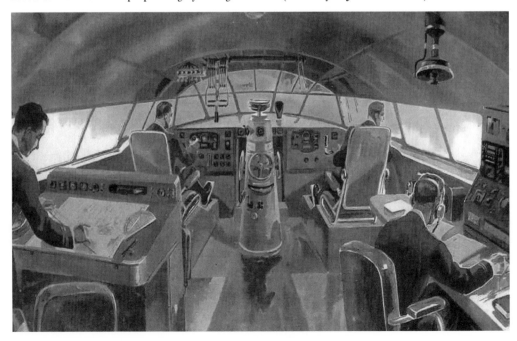

Porte des Hourtiquets, Lake Biscarosse. (Main photos © Ville de Biscarosse–Musée de l'Hydraviation)

Germany

In November 1922 the all-metal Dornier Wal (Whale) emerged from the Marina di Pisa factory in Italy, featuring a tandem-engine configuration and sponsons rather than wing floats. Deutsche Luft Hansa began flying to Oslo in 1927, by which time production had opened at Manzel in Germany.

In 1929, the twelve-engined Dornier Do X emerged from Altenrhein as the world's largest aeroplane. A year later it crossed to New York and returned to Lake Müggelsee in 1932. Underpowered and uneconomical, it never conquered the Atlantic and lasted less than a year with Lufthansa.

Blohm und Voss had worked towards the same goal but, by September 1940, when the *Viking* made its first flight, Germany was again at war. Powered by six diesel engines, it should have made a name for itself as a transatlantic airliner. Instead it was passed to the Luftwaffe.

Dornier Wal, Gressholmen, 1930. (© Fotoarkivet Norske Teknisk Museum)

Pisa-built I-DEOR pictured at Stromness, 1924, while surveying a North Atlantic service.
(© Orkney Archive and Library)

Dornier Do X at Lake Müggelsee near Berlin. (© Dornier Museum, Friedrichshafen (Airbus Group))

Italy

Used on early services, elderly biplane Cant flying boats were replaced by Dornier Wal, Super Wal and Savoia Marchetti flying boats but, in 1934, all four airlines – Aero Espresso Italiano (AEI), Società Aerea Mediterranea (SAM), Società Anonima Navigazione Aerea (SANA) and Società Italiana Servizi Aerei (SISA) – merged to form Ala Littoria. From 1940, when Italy entered the war, flying boats were used as military transports.

Above: Corporatión Sudamericana Macchi M.C. 94. (Courtesy of Archivo General de la Nación Argentina MC-94 11)

Left: Società Anonima di Navigazione Aerea Dornier R4 Superwal. (Courtesy of European Airlines)

Norway

The three Channel flying boats of Det Norske Luftfartsrederi were the first in Norway. Deutsche Luft Hansa AG later replaced their Wal flying boats with larger capacity Junkers 52 floatplanes, the summer service flown by Det Norske Luftfartselskap A/S Fred Olsen. The summer service was known as the Midnattssolruten – Midnight Sun Route.

DNL timetable cover, showing Skomvaer lighthouse in the Lofoten Islands.
(© SAS Museum, Gardermoen, Norway)

Pan Am's decision to fly a Newfoundland-Foynes route ended DNL's hopes of a Reykjavik-Bergen service and Sikorsky S-43 *Valkyrien* was stored at Malmö until June 1937, when a shortlived service began to Stockholm. Sold to Aéromaritime, the Sikorsky joined four others in flying coastal services through French West Africa, south of Dakar.

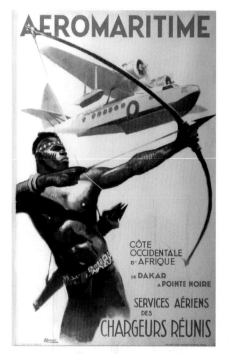

Left: (Courtesy of Onslows Auctioneers via Millers Antiques)

Below: Gressholmen 1936. (© Norsk Teknisk Museum/ Teigens Fotoatelier)

Australia

By September 1938 the Empire Air Mail Service included India, Malaya, Australia, New Zealand and Hong Kong. Qantas crews flew to Singapore.

Coolangatta and *Cooee*, Rose Bay, June 1936. (© State Library of New South Wales)

Camilla and *Coriolanus*, Rose Bay terminal, opened 4 August 1938. (© Milton Kent and Civil Aviation Historical Society, Melbourne)

New Zealand

New Zealand, Australia and the UK formed Tasman Empire Airways (TEAL) to fly between New Zealand and Australia. *Awarua* landed at Waitemata harbour on 3 April 1939. Damaged en route, *Australia* was rebuilt and retained as *Clare*. *Aotearoa* arrived on 28 August but six days later the United Kingdom was at war.

Captain Burgess with crew at Southampton. (Courtesy of Springbourne Library, Bournemouth)

Aotearoa cocktail
bar, circa 1941.

Aotearoa, 18 June 1945. The thousandth crossing of the Tasman Sea.
(© Alexander Turnbull Library WA–01302–G)

Britain at War

In September 1939, Imperial Airways moved its flying boats to Poole Harbour in Dorset. However, *Corsair* had failed to arrive at Juba in March. Replacement direction-finding equipment was fitted, but not tested, before leaving Kisumu on Lake Victoria, and a search in misty conditions had ended on the river Dungu, near the village of Faradje in the Belgian Congo, some 200 miles west of Juba. The passengers and mail were sent on overland. A salvage team sent by Shorts found that the partially-submerged flying boat was repairable, but an attempt to leave in July again ended at the river bank with a fresh hole in the hull.

Corsair finally escaped on 6 January 1940, after the hull was rebuilt and the water level was raised by building a dam – incredible undertakings in the jungle. The local workers soon found use for the discarded metal and upholstery, while the mud huts erected to house them all became known as Corsairville.

Imperial Airways *Corsair* at Hythe, possibly on returning from Faradje. (Bob Winkworth collection)

BOAC Poole

Having pioneered services across Europe to the Far East for an incredibly short two years, Imperial Airways was officially absorbed by BOAC on 1 April 1940. An eight-year association with Poole saw passenger-handling facilities moved from Airways House (now Poole Museum) to the Carter Pottery premises on the quayside and, ultimately, to a Marine Terminal at Salterns Way, Lilliput. The call up of men for the services saw young women trained to ferry passengers and engineers by launch to and from the moorings.

Above: Marinecraft Unit Seawomen Isobel Rickard, Mary Hill, Bosun Frank Hewitt, Bunny Reece, Molly Skinner, Nora Bevis and Eileen Wigg.

Right: Former pottery paintress Mollie Skinner. Lapel badges show proficiency in semaphore and morse.

Mollie Skinner with ENSA entertainer George Formby and his wife Beryl. (Courtesy of Mrs Mollie Harman née Skinner)

Eighteen-year-old Eileen Wigg ferried singer and 'Forces Sweetheart' Vera Lynn to her flying boat and remembered General Montgomery bringing them back bananas, a luxury in wartime Britain.

(Courtesy of Mrs Eileen Armstrong née Wigg)

Horseshoe Route

Britain was isolated from Europe, save for the vital Poole-Lisbon flying boat service which connected with the Pan American Clippers. But from July 1940, crews flew from Durban to Cairo to link with the pre-war Empire route to Australia, known as the 'Horseshoe Route', due to its appearance on a map. From July 1941, the West Africa route extended eastwards to link with the Horseshoe.

On finishing a tour with 70 Squadron at Kabrit, Jim Peers completed a conversion course at Vaaldam and joined the crews flying from Durban to Calcutta. Qantas crews flew on to Australia and New Zealand.

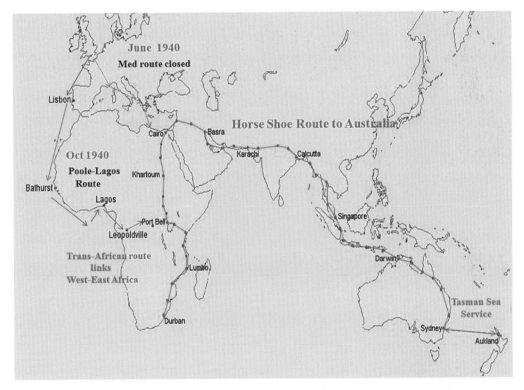

(From author's collection)

Jim Peers. (Courtesy of Mrs Jean Peers)

Flying over the Vaaldam. (Courtesy of Captain Jim Peers)

Boeing 314A

With the American Atlantic service ending in neutral Ireland, a shuttle was flown between Poole and Foynes. BOAC's Subsidiary Airways (Atlantic) bought three longer-range Boeing 314As for over £250,000 each and, from initially flying the Foynes–Lisbon–Lagos West Africa route, from December 1941 *Bristol*, *Berwick* and *Bangor* began crossing the Atlantic to America.

Bangor at Baltimore, BOAC's maintenance base.

(Photos courtesy of Boeing specialist navigator
Vic Pitcher)

Catalina to India

The need to resume contact between Australia and London saw a fleet of Qantas Catalinas flying diplomatic mail between the Swan river in Western Australia and Lake Koggala, Ceylon, from June 1943. Despite the extra fuel tanks, the interior was fitted with three chairs, occupied by military officers in civilian clothes. The world's longest passenger service, it was noisy, and you couldn't smoke. But the view of the starlit night skies was memorable, provided you ignored having to cross enemy-held islands in blackout conditions.

Having endured more than twenty-four hours in the air, passengers received a certificate admitting them to the secret 'Order of the Double Sunrise'. Employed in doping the fabric of wartime civilian flying boats at Rose Bay, Ruth Wiseman had fortunately kept a snapshot of Catalina 3 *Rigel Star*.

Catalina 5 *Spica Star*, Swan river, Western Australia. (Unknown)

Rigel Star, Rose Bay. (Courtesy of Captain Henry de Courcier)

Transport Sunderlands

With air transport needed to support the battles in North Africa, Short Brothers began converting military Sunderland III flying boats for BOAC and the RAF. From March 1943, transport Sunderlands operated the Poole-Lagos-West Africa service via Foynes, Bathurst and Freetown. Though within RAF Transport Command, BOAC retained its own identity.

BOAC Seawomen with Transport Sunderland III. (Courtesy of Chaz Bowyer)

ZC and ZH (later *Hamilton* and *Harwich*) Poole, circa 1945. (Courtesy of Richard Riding)

Post-war

From 1945 transport Sunderlands were upgraded to Hythe-class airliner standard, given sixteen seats, a promenade deck and upgraded engines. Three extra dinghies were stowed aboard. The nose turret remained, but the rear turret was faired over to avoid delay.

Joe Parker and Lawrence Glover aboard *Hythe*. (Courtesy of Philip Glover)

Hailsham safely beached near Brownsea Island, Poole after losing a wing float – before tide returned. (Courtesy of Mrs Mollie Harman)

Golden Hind, Durban, circa 1947. (© Nicole White, grand-daughter of Captain Roger Mollard)

A sad end for the G-class flagship. (K.C.Sherris)

Retired from BOAC service in 1947, *Golden Hind* was bought by Fleet Airways and flown from Poole to the Medway. It never flew again and was finally moored on the Swale in sight of the Harty Ferry Inn until dismantled around 1954.

One that Got Away

Short's new civil design, the Sandringham, proved popular across the world but was soon replaced by the Solent.

Sandringham 7 *St George* was bought for £20,000 by Captain P.G. Taylor. Refitted by Saunders-Roe in Cowes, *Frigate Bird III* left for Australia in 1954, the year he was knighted.

Flown personally by Sir Gordon on Pacific Island cruises from Sydney until 1958 and subsequently retired by TAI, *Le Bermuda* was saved from dereliction in 1978 and shipped to le Musée de l'air at le Bourget.

Sandringhams awaiting scrapping, Hamworthy, Dorset, 1949. (From author's collection)

Portsmouth and *Penzance* (nearest camera), 1954. (Courtesy of John Newall)

St George with Sally Coleman. (© Ivor Coleman)

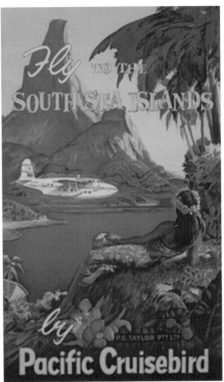

Above left: Captain (Sir) P.J. Taylor. (© Collection Powerhouse Museum, Sydney)

Above right: His 'air cruise' charters poster. (© Family of Sir Gordon Taylor via Museum of Sydney)

Last Days at Poole

Post-war economies (launches were expensive) saw BOAC move from Poole to Southampton where a new terminal opened in 1948 for a Solent *Springbok* service to Africa.

BOAC Marine Terminal building, Salterns Way, Lilliput, Poole.

Parkstone Yacht Club with Hythe *Harlequin* and Sandringham *Portmarnock*. (Author's collection)

Springbok Service

Solent 2 *Salisbury*,
believed to
be piloted by
Captain Baker.

Solent 2 *Scapa*, Southampton. (*Salisbury* and *Scapa* photos courtesy of Bob Raynor)

Captain Rose at the bar of BOAC Solent. (© Rose collection)

Smoking was
still allowed.
(© Rose collection)

East Africa

On 3 November 1949, the first Solent service landed on Lake Nyasa from Johannesburg. Seven days later the first diversionary service arrived from Southampton. From then on, one of the three weekly services to Vaaldam arrived on Tuesday, followed on Thursday by the return flight to Southampton.

Solent *Salcombe*, Lake Nyasa, November 1949.

(Lake Nyasa
© David Rose,
BOAC
coxswain)

A December 1949 flight to Lake Navaisha, Kenya, by Kathleen Lenham, who had accepted a teaching post at Kongwa (now Mnyakongo Primary School) provided colourful memories of her time aboard Solent 3 *City of Belfast* flown by Captain Rotherham. The return of *Somerset* from Johannesburg on 14 November 1950 ended BOAC flying-boat operations.

Left: Kathleen Lenham.

Below: Crossing the Equator Certificate.

BOAC Speedbird folder.

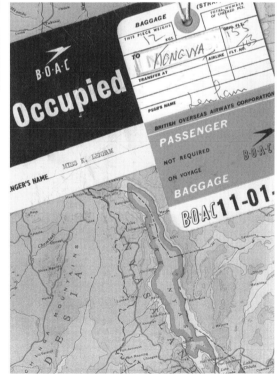

Passenger documentation and map folder.

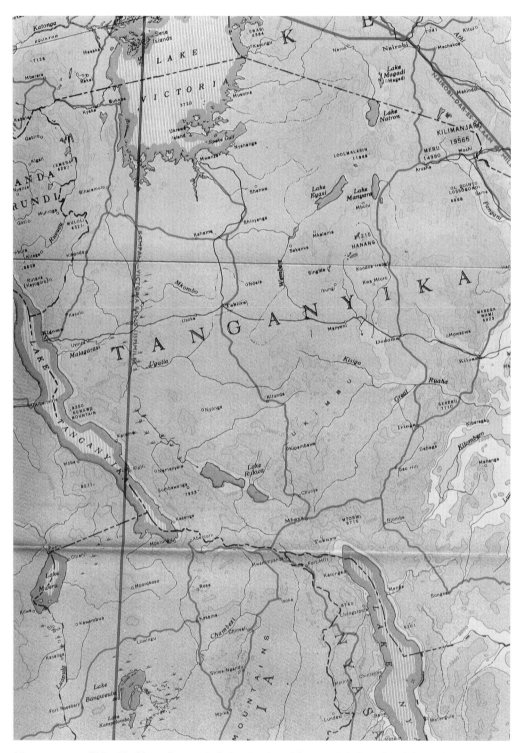

Map courtesy of Mrs Kathleen Gurney (née Lenham) and her son BA Captain Richard Gurney.

Aquila

Formed by former RAF Sunderland pilot Barry Aikman, Aquila Airways continued to operate civilian Sunderland and Solent flying boats until 30 September 1958 when the return of *Awatere* from Madeira ended all British commercial flying-boat services.

Solent 3 *City of Funchal*, Madeira. (© José Carvalho)

Solents *Solway* and *City of Liverpool*, pictured in Hamworthy after a failed coffee-bar project. (Author's collection)

The Giants

Intended to fly wartime troops direct to Europe, the H-4 Hercules or 'Spruce Goose', built of laminated birch, had eventually left the surface of Long Beach Harbour, California, in 1947, piloted by millionaire owner Howard Hughes. It was stored at an estimated cost of $1 million a year until his death in 1976.

Born of BOAC's interest in three post-war transatlantic flying boats, the Saunders-Roe *Princess* flew in August 1952, by which time the airline had lost interest and development costs had risen to £10 million. The flying example and two airframes were scrapped for a fraction of the cost.

Spruce Goose.
(© Evergreen
Aviation and
Space Museum,
Oregon)

Princess. Built
at Cowes, Isle
of Wight.
(© Dave Fagan.
Hampshire
Airfields)

Madeira

With the end of Aquila, two former US Navy Martin Mariners were converted for airline service by Aero-Topográficia SA. *Madeira* flew the first passengers to Funchal on 1 October 1958 but services were cancelled after the loss of *Porto Santo*. A Constellation of Transportes Aeros Portugueses resumed communication by air in July 1964 after a runway was built on the east coast of the island.

Mariner on arrival at Lisbon. (© José Mergulhão)

Refurbished cabin.
(© José Mergulhão)

Porto Santo, Funchal harbour. (© José Carvalho)

Norway

From 1947, three Short Sandringham 6 flying boats, built expressly for Det Norske Luftfartselskap A/S (DNL), were flying an Oslo/Fornebu-Tromsø summer service. *Kvitbjørn*, *Bukken Bruse* and *Bamse Brakar* became known as 'Flying Steamers' and were supplemented by *Jutulen* and *Polar Bjørn*.

Bamse Brakar ('Teddy Bear' Brakar). (Unknown/ Norwegian Museum)

In full flow. (Courtesy of The Nostalgic Picture Library)

South America

Over 30,000 people watched Sandringham *Argentina* arrive over Buenos Aires in November 1945, the first of the converted Sunderlands flown from Belfast for the Compañía Argentina de Aeronavegación, owned by millionaire Alberto Dodero. Absorbed within the Sociedad Mixa Aviacon del Lotoralt Fluvial Argentina in 1946, flying boats continued in Uruguay until around 1962. They lasted longer in Argentina, where the four regional airlines were absorbed by Aerolinas Argentinas. Briefly operated as transports by the Cooperativa Argentina de Aeronavegantes, the last were broken up at Basin F, Puerto Neuvo, around January 1967.

Sandringham 2 *Uruguay.*
(Courtesy of Carlos Mey)

New Zealand

Replaced by four Sandringham 4s, *Awarua* and *Aotearoa* were retired from the Tasman Sea service in 1947. Displayed within a secure waterfront enclosure at Mission Bay, *Aotearoa* survived until 1950.

It was a pity nobody saved the nose section. (© Marcus Bridle/Peter Lewis)

(© MOTAT Library)

Finally operated by four Solent flying boats, the Auckland-Sydney crossing was reduced to under six hours. With DC-6 airliners taking over the Wellington-Sydney service, *Aranui* ended the Tahiti-Auckland service in September 1960 and has been lovingly preserved at Auckland's Museum of Transport and Technology.

South Pacific Air Lines
Having ended Trans-Oceanic Airways in 1953, Bryan Monkton formed South Pacific Airlines, with the intention of flying a Honolulu-Tahiti service via Christmas Island

(Courtesy of Oakland
Aviation Museum)

with three Solent flying boats. The UK's intention to use the island as an atomic test site ended everything.

Subsequently sold for scrap, *Isle of Tahiti*, bought by Seaflite Oceanographic owners Rick and Randy Grant, was refurbished and appeared in *Raiders of the Lost Ark* with Harrison Ford taking a window seat. It is seen today at Oakland Aviation Museum in its former BOAC livery as *City of Cardiff*.

Solent 3 *City of Cardiff.*
Oakland Aviation Museum.
(© Joseph May Travel for
Aircraft)

Australia

Situated some 370 miles off the eastern seaboard of Australia, by the 1930s Lord Howe
Island had become a popular tourist resort. With post-war flying-boat operations
restricted to island charters to avoid competition with landplanes, services were
operated by Qantas, Trans-Oceanic Airways, Barrier Reef Airways and Ansett until
1974 when a runway was built for Lord Howe Island Airport.

Princess of Cairns, Hayman Island, May 1951. (Unknown)

Ansett *Beachcomber* and *Islander* off Lord Howe Island. (© Frank Stamford)

Bought by Captain Charles Blair for Antilles Air Boats, the departure of *Excalibur VIII*, the former *Islander*, from Rose Bay in September and *Southern Cross* (*Beachcomber*) in November 1974 effectively ended Australian commercial flying-boat services.

End of an Era

Formed in 1964 by retired USAF Brigadier General and Pan Am senior pilot Charles Blair, Antilles Air Boats were soon making 120 flights a day around the Virgin Islands from St Croix. In 1968, the pilot married Hollywood film star Maureen O'Hara who subsequently became company director.

(© Jim Cole. 1969, 2011 Stars and Stripes)

Grumman
Goose Charlotte
Amalies Harbour.
(© Mick Bajcar)

Return to Poole

In 1976 *Southern Cross* was flown from St Croix to Ireland for the first of two seasons with Aer Arann and whilst there was invited to return to Poole, from where Captain 'Tommy' Rose had delivered the Tasman-class Sandringham 4 to TEAL as *Auckland* in 1947.

Captain H.J. Rose, BOAC Marine Terminal, Lilliput.

Auckland, Mechanics Bay, 1947. (© Rose Collection)

Sandbanks Chain Ferry, August 1976. (Courtesy of Bob Rayner)

Southern Cross moored off Studland Beach, Dorset. (Author's collection)

Poole Harbour. Noel Holle refuelling–800 gallons in 30 minutes.

The view from mooring to Sandbanks Hotel. (Author's collection)

The view from Poole Harbour mooring to Brownsea Island.

Solent Sky
Bought for the nation in 1982, *Southern Cross* is displayed as *Beachcomber* at Solent Sky Museum, Southampton.

(Author's Collection)

Fantasy of Flight, Florida

Following the death of Charles Blair, *Excalibur VIII*, the former *Islander*, was sold to Edward Hulton who subsequently sold the last airworthy civilian Sunderland V to Kermit Weeks' Fantasy of Flight Museum in Florida.

July 1993, Goodbye Calshot. (Courtesy of Colin Lee)

A new Home in Florida. (© Kermit Weeks' Fantasy of Flight)

Africa Safari Company

The brainchild of safari guide Pierre Jaunet, the use of a flying boat for an aerial safari of Africa provided memorable experiences for those applying to Bushbuck Safaris until 1994, when Z-Cat was sold to the Catalina Club of New Zealand. They display their charge as XX-T of 6 Squadron RNZAF.

Above left: Aircraft logo in Africa. *On right*: Pierre and Antoinette Jaunet. (© Pierre Jaunet)

Lake Malawi, Tanzania, 1990. (© Tim Spearman)

(© Phillip Treweek)

Foynes Flying-Boat Museum

On 9 July 1989, the fiftieth anniversary of the arrival of *Yankee Clipper* from New York, Maureen O'Hara Blair officially opened the Foynes Flying Boat Museum. In 2002 the museum bought the entire terminal building which now features the rebuilt air traffic control tower and a unique full-size replica of the Boeing flying boat.

(© Foynes Flying Boat Museum)

Poole Flying Boats Celebration
During eight-and-a-half years of flying boat operations, over 34,000 passengers had flown into Poole. Not a single passenger was injured and only *Maia* was lost (sunk), due to enemy action. Formed in 2006 to remind people of those highly successful years, Poole Flying Boats Celebration has achieved charity status with Lady Nadine Cobham welcomed as patron.

The blue plaque installed at the former Marine Terminal, Lilliput.

Storyboard at harbourside promenade with David Rose, Vic Pitcher, John Witcomb. (© Leslie Dawson)

International Seaplane Air Show

Since 1991 the bi-annual air show held at Lake Biscarosse, home to the Musée de l'Hydraviation, has attracted repeat visits by the sole Do 24ATT restored by Irén Dornier, grandson of Professor Claudius Dornier, and the PBY-5A of Plane Sailing based at Duxford.

(© Dr Andreas Zeitler)

Plane Sailing Catalina over Musée de l'hydraviation, Lake Biscarosse.
(© Collection Musée de l'Hydraviation. Origine Pierre Fontaine, 2010)

Passenger Flying Boat Fleets

Bermuda and West Atlantic Aviation Company
Supermarine Channel 1 G-EAEF, EG, EJ.

British Marine Air Navigation Company/ Imperial Airways
Supermarine Sea Eagle G-EBFK, BGR, BGS.

Imperial Airways
Short Calcutta-class
   City of Rome; City of Khartoum; City of Salonika; City of Alexandria; City of Athens.

Short Kent-class   *Scipio, Sylvanus, Satyrus*

Imperial Airways
Short C-class 'Empire'
   S–23: *Canopus, Caledonia, Centaurus, Cavalier, Cambria, Castor, Cassiopeia, Capella, Cygnus, Capricornus, Corsair, Courtier, Challenger, Centurion, Coriolanus, Calpurnia, Ceres, Clio, Circe, Calypso, Camilla, Corinna, Cordelia, Cameronian, Corinthian, Coogee, Corio, Coorong, Carpentaria, Coolangatta, Cooee, Champion.,* S–30: *Cabot, Caribou, Connnemara, Clyde, Aotearoa, Australia, Awarua, Cathay, Clifton.* S–33: *Cleopatra.*

Short S-26 G-class *Golden Hind; Golden Fleece; Golden Horn.*

BOAC Model 28/Catalina *Catalina Guba.*
                     Vega Star; Altair Star; Rigel Star;
                     Antares Star; Spica Star.   to Qantas

BOAC Hythe-class Transport Sunderland 3
   G-AGIB, GET, GKX, *Hailsham, Hamble, Hamilton, Hanwell, Harlequin, Honduras, Harwich, Haslemere, Halstead, Hungerford, Hadfield, Hawkesbury, Henley, Hunter, Hanbury*   to RAF
   Huntingdon, Hotspur   Belfast
   Hampshire, Hudson, Howard, Hobart, Hythe, Helmsdale.   Aquila

Sandringham 1 *Himalaya*   to Aquila
Remainder built Belfast.

Plymouth-class Sandringham 5
        Portland, Portsmouth, Penzance, Portsea, Pembroke,
        Perth, Pevensey, Portmarnock, Poole.   to Qantas

Bermuda-class Sandringham 7
        Saint Andrew; Saint David.   to CAUSA
        Saint George sold P.G. Taylor   RAI
        ***Musée de l'air et d'espace, le Bourget.**

Solent 2   *Severn, Solway, Stornoway, Sark, Scarborough*
        returned Ministry of Supply
        Salcombe, Somerset   to TOA
        Southampton   Aquila
        Salisbury, Sussex, Scapa converted to Mk 3 renamed
        Southsea   converted to Mk 3

Solent 3   *City of Edinburgh* (sunk)
        City of Salisbury; City of York; Southsea
        returned Ministry of Supply
        City of Liverpool   to MAEE
        City of Belfast   TEAL
        City of London; City of Cardiff   TOA
        Singapore   SPAL
        trainer G-AGWU   Aquila (G-ANAJ)

Boeing 314A   *Berwick, Bangor, Bristol*   to World Airways

AQUILA
Hythe-class Transport Sunderland 3
        Hunter, Halstead, Hawkesbury, Henley, Hobart, Hythe, Helmsdale
        Haslemere, Hamble, Hudson, Hungerford, Hampshire, Hadfield.

AQUILA
Sunderland 3s replaced by
Sandringham 1   *Himalaya*
Solent 2   *Southampton*

Solent 3   *City of Funchal; Sydney*
Solent 4   *Awatere, Aotearoa II.*
                  Return of Awatere (30 September 1958) ended UK passenger services.

PORTUGAL
Aero-Topográfica SA
Martin Mariner 5.   *Porto Santo; Madeira.*

FRANCE
Aéromaritime
Sikorsky S-38   F-AOUC
Sikorsky S-43   F-OUK, UL, UM, QHY, REX *Valkyrien*
                  Ceased operations in 1944/45

Air France
Loiré et Olivier H242
Ville de Cannes; Ville de Bone; Ville de Tunis; Ville d'Algiers; Ville d'Oran; Ville de Marseille; Ville d'Ajaccio; Ville de Tripoli; Ville de Beyrouth; Ville de Toulon; Ville de Nice; Ville de Bizerte; Ville de Casablanca; Ville de Rabat.

Latécoère L300 *Croix du Sud*

Latécoère L301 *Ville de Buenos Aires; Ville de Rio; Ville de Janeiro; Ville de Santiago; Ville de Chile.*

Latécoère
L631					
01	Latécoère		Luftwaffe 63+11.	
02	Air France	*Lionel de Marmier*	France-Hydro	stored
03	Air France	*Henry Guillaumet*	SeMAF	
04	Air France		SeMAF France-Hydro	
05	Air France		France-Hydro	stored
06	Air France			
07	Latécoère			
08	Air France		France-Hydro	stored
09, 10				stored
11	Air France		SeMAF France-Hydro	stored

GERMANY
Deutsche Luft Hansa AG Stettin/Lubeck to Oslo 1927-1934
Dornier Wal *Bremerhaven, Flensburg, Hai, Hecht, Helgoland, Lübeck Sägefisch, Thunfisch,* D-1213, D-1488.

SuperWal	*Graf Zeppelin; Hugo Eckener/Blauwal; Narwal, Pottwal.*
Rohrbach Ro V trainer	*Rocco* lent May/June 1928

NORWAY
Det Norske Luftfartsrederi A/S

Supermarine Channel 1	N-9,	N-10,	N-11	sold
Friedrichshafen FF49C	N-6,	N-8,	N-3	sold

Ceased operating Oct 1920

Det Norske Luftfartselskap A/S Fred. Olsen and Bergenske

Sikorsky S-43	*Valkyrien*	**to** Aeromaritime

Vingtor Luftveier

Catalina	*Vingtor*	
	JX381	**to** Royal Norwegian Air Force

Det Norske Luftfartselskap (DNL) merged SAS 1949

Sandringham 6	*Bamse Brakar; Bukken Bruse; Jutulen, Kvitbjørn.*	
	Polar Bjørn	**to** Aerolineas Argentinas.

ITALY
Ala Littoria

Macchi MC-94	I-NEPI
absorbed Luftwaffe	I-ARNO/D-ADQN, ENZA/ADQS, LIRI/ ADQO, NARO/ADQR, NETO/D-ADQT, SILE/ ADQQ, TOCE/ADQP,
	ANIO, LATO, NEVA **to** Corporation Sudamericana.

SA Navigazione Aerea (SANA)

Dornier R2 Wal *Cabina*	
	I-AYZY, YZZ, ZDI, ZDL, ZDQ, ZDZ, ZEF, ZER, CITO, D-AOK, AUR, EAR, OAR.
Superwal R4	I –RATA, ENE, EOS, IDE, ONY, UDO.

Savoia-Marchetti Sm.66

I- AABF, ALGA, ALTE, BLEO, EGEO, FBAA, LIDO, MIRA, NAVE, NEMI, PRUA, REDI, RIVA, SOLA, VALE, VELA.

Societè Aerea Mediterranea
Savoia-Marchetti S.55

I- AABC, AABE, AABF, AABG, NDRA, OLAO, OLCO, RZIO, SILI, STRO, TACO.

*Private S-55 Jahú I-BAUQ displayed at Museu Transportes, in São Paulo, Brazil.

URUGUAY
La Compañía Aeronáutica Uruguaya S.A. (CAUSA) Montevideo

Ju 52/3m	*El Uruguayo*	* **Museo Aeronautico**
Ju 52/3m	*El Argentino*	
Sandringham 7 (*Saint Andrew*)	unnamed	
Civ.Sunderland (*Rio de la Plata*)	*General Artigas*	
Civ.Sunderland (DP195)	*Capitan Boiso Lanza*	
Civ.Sunderland (ML876)	*General San Martin*	
Sandringham 7 (*Saint David*)	unnamed	

Flying boat services ended in May 1962

ARGENTINA
Corporación Sudamericana de Servicios Aéreos

MC.94 (I-ANIO)	*Rio de la Plata*	to Dodero /ALFA
MC.94 (I-NEVA)	*Rio Parana,*	to ALFA
MC.94 (I-LATO)	unnamed	to ALFA
Civ.Sunderland (ML876)	*Rio de la Plata*	to CAUSA

Compañía Argentina de Aeronavegación Dodero SA

MC.94	*Rio de la Plata*	
MC.94	*Rio Parana*	
MC.94	unnamed	
Sandringham 2 (DD834)	*Uruguay*	
Sandringham 2 (DV964)	*Argentina*	to Aerolinas Argentinas.
Sandringham 3 (DD841)	*Brasil*	Aero.Arg.
Sandringham 3 (EJ170)	*Inglaterra*	Aero.Arg.
Sandringham 2 (ML843)	*Paraguay*	Aero.Arg.

Aerolineas Argentinas

Sandringham 3 (DD841)	*Brasil*	
Civ.Sunderland (EK579)	*Uruguay*	
Civ.Sunderland (EJ 171)	*Rio de la Plata*	to Cooperative. Argentina
Sandringham 2 (DV964)	*Argentina*	Coop. Arg.
Sandringham 3 (EJ 170)	*Inglaterra*	Coop. Arg.
Sandringham 2 (ML 843)	*Paraguay*	Coop. Arg.
Sandringham 6 (JM714)	*Polar Bjørn*	Coop. Arg. *Almirante Zar*

Cooperativa Argentina de Aeronavegantes

Sandringham 2	*Rio Aguilero*	renamed *Argentina*
Sandringham 3	*Inglaterra*	renamed *Provincia de Formoza*
Sandringham 2	*Paraguay*	
Sandringham 6	*Almirante Zar*	
Civ.Sunderland	*Rio de la Plata*	

NEW ZEALAND
TEAL Tasman Sea Service

(*Cumberland renamed in factory*)	S-30	*Aotearoa*
(*Captain Cook renamed in factory*)	S-30	*Awarua*

Training/route-proving Catalinas

NZ4038/ZK-AMI	returned RNZAF
NZ4035/ ZK-AMP	returned RNZAF

Replaced 1946/7 by
Tasman-class Sandringham 4

	Tasman	(ML761)	to Qantas
	Australia	(NJ255)	Qantas
	New Zealand	(NJ 179)	
	Auckland	(JM 175)	to Barrier Reef

Solent 4

Aparimu	(Mk 3 *City of Belfast*)	
Ararangi		
Aotearoa II		to Aquila
Awatere		Aquila

Aranui * **Museum of Transport and Technology, Auckland**

AUSTRALIA
Qantas /QEA six C-class to operate Singapore-Sydney route.

Corio		to Imperial Airways
Coorong		Imperial Airways
Carpentaria	stranded	to BOAC
Cooee	stranded	BOAC
Camilla	absorbed after the fall of Singapore VH-ADU	
Circe	absorbed	
Corinna	absorbed	
Corinthian	absorbed	

Coriolanus	absorbed VH–ABG	
Centaurus		to RAAF A18-10
Calypso		RAAF A18-11
Coogee		RAAF A18-12
Coolangatta		RAAF A18-13
Clifton		RAAF

Long-Range 'Double Sunrise' Catalina fleet

Vega Star (1); *Altair Star* (2); *Rigel Star* (3); *Antares Star* (4); *Spica Star* (5).

Lord Howe Island Catalina Service

(JX635) VH-EAX
(JX662) VH-EAW

Sandringham	Mk 4	(*Tasman*)	unnamed	
	Mk 5	(*Portmarnock*)	*Pacific Warrior*	
	Mk 5	(*Pevensey*)	*Pacific Explorer*	
	Mk 5	(*Poole*)	**Pacific Chieftain**	to Ansett

Barrier Reef Airways

Sandringham 4	(*New Zealand*)	*Princess of Cairns*	
Catalina	(JZ834)	*Beachcomber*	
Catalina	(JZ838)	*Buccaneer*	
Sandringham 4	(*Aucklamd*)	**Beachcomber**	to Ansett

Sir Gordon Taylor Air Cruises

Sandringham 7	(*Saint George*)	*Frigate Bird III*	to TAI

Transports Aeriens Intercontineaux (TAI)

Sandringham 7	(*Frigate Bird III*) unnamed	to RAI

Resaau Aeriens Interinsulaire (RAI)

Sandringham 7	'Le Bermuda'	***Musée de l'air et d'espace, le Bourget**

Trans-Oceanic Airways

Sunderland 3	(ML731)	*Pacific Star*
Sunderland 3	(ML733)	*Australis*
Solent 2	(*Salcombe*)	*Star of Hobart*
Solent 3	(*City of London*)	unnamed

Sunderland 3	(ML734)	*Tahiti Star*	to Ansett
Solent 2	(*Somerset*)	unnamed	SPAL
Solent 3	(*City of Cardiff*)	*Star of Papua*	SPAL

Ansett Flying Boat Services

Sunderland 3		*Tahiti Star*
Sandringham 4		*Pacific Chieftain*
Sandringham 4		*Beachcomber*	to Antilles
Sunderland V	(ML814)	*Islander*	Antilles

AMERICA
Aeromarine West Indies Airways/ Aeromarine Airways

Curtiss Model 75 *Balboa, Buckeye, Columbas, Cordeaux (Mendoza), Nina, Pinta, Ponce de León; Santa Maria, Wolverine.*

Model 85 *Ambassador, Biltmore, Florida, McAlpin, Miami, Morro Castle; Niagara, New Jersey; New York; Pennsylvania, Presidente Zayas; Ritz- Carlton; Vanderbilt, Virginia, Waldorf.*

New York, Rio, and Buenos Aires Line (NYRBA)

Consolidated

Commodore *Argentina, Cuba, Havana, Miami, Puerto Rico; New York; Rio de Janeiro; Trinidad, Uruguay,* NC667M unnamed,

Sikorsky 38A *Washington, Montevideo.*

38B NC73K, NC113, 943, 944, 946M, NC301, 302, 308N.

absorbed Pan American Airways

Pan American Airways

Consolidated Commodore NYRBA fleet + NC669, 670M

Sikorsky S-38A NC8000, 8020, 8044.

Sikorsky 38B NC197H, 74, 75K, NC3V, 16-19, 21, 22, 40V 113, 142-146, 300- 302, 304-6-8-9, 945M, NC9107, 137, 151, 9775, 9776.

Douglas Dolphin NC-14239 (' 21'), 14240 ('22').

Sikorsky S-40 Clippers	*American, Caribbean, Southern.*	to U.S.N
S-42.	*Brazilian, West Indies,* NC–824M.	
S-42A.	*Dominican, Jamaica, Antilles, Brazilian.*	

S-42B.	*Pan American II;* renamed *Samoan; Bermuda,* renamed *Alaska, Hong Kong II.*		
	Pan American III; renamed *Bermuda.*		

Martin 130 Clippers	*Hawaii, Philippine, China.*		

Boeing B.314 Clippers	*Honolulu*		
	Yankee	operated for USN	
	Atlantic	operated for USN	
	Dixie	operated for USN	to World Airways
	California	to USN	World Airways
	American	to USN	World Airways
314A Clippers	*Pacific*	to USN	Universal Airlines
	Capetown	to USN	American International
	Anzac	to USN	American Intn – World Airways

American Export/Overseas Airlines
Sikorsky VS-44A

	Excalibur	
	Exeter	to Transporte Aéreo de Carga Internacional
	Excambian	Avalon Air Transport - Antilles

South Pacific Air Lines
Solent 3 (*Singapore*)   unnamed
Solent 2 (*Somerset)*   unnamed
Solent 3 (*City of Cardiff*)   *Isle of Tahiti*   sold to Grant Bros
*displayed as *City of Cardiff* at Oakland Aviation Museum

PRIVATE
Douglas Dolphin 117   *Rover* owned William (Bill) Boeing
*U.S. National Museum of Naval Aviation, Pensacola, Florida.

Sikorsky S-38 BS   *Osas Ark* owned Martin and Osa Johnson   to Aero Inter-Americano SA

S-39CS   *Spirit of Africa* Martin and Osa Johnson   to Civil Air Guard
*S38 and S39 replicas, Fantasy of Flight Museum Florida

VIRGIN ISLES Antilles Air Boats

Sikorsky VS–44A	*Excambian*	gifted to the Naval Aviation Museum

* **New England Air Museum**

Sandringham 4	*Southern Cross*	bought by the Science Museum

* **displayed Solent Sky Museum as** *Beachcomber*

Civil Sunderland (ML 814/ *Islander*)	*Excalibur VIII*	stored	bought by Edward Hulton

* **sold to Kermit Weeks' Fantasy of Flight Museum, Florida**